Ten P[illegible]
about M[illegible]

Candlestick Press

Published by:
Candlestick Press,
Diversity House, 72 Nottingham Road, Arnold, Nottingham NG5 6LF, UK
www.candlestickpress.co.uk

Printed by Ratcliff & Roper Print Group, Nottinghamshire, UK

Reprinted 2011, 2012, 2014, 2015, 2016, 2017, 2018

ISBN 978 1 907598 03 6

Dedicated to the memory of Susan Milne (1923 - 2007)

Acknowledgements:
Candlestick Press thanks Bloodaxe Books for permission to reprint Maura Dooley, 'Mirror' (from *Sound Barrier*, Bloodaxe Books, 2002), Fleur Adcock, 'The Chiffonier' (from *Poems 1960 - 2000*, Bloodaxe Books, 2000) and Jackie Kay, 'I try my absolute best' (from *Darling: New and Selected Poems*, Bloodaxe Books, 2007); Gillian Clarke and Carcanet Press for 'The Habit of Light' (from *Collected Poems*,1997); Jenny Joseph for 'Going out with Mum' from *All The Things I See* (Macmillan Children's Books, 2000). 'Mrs Gilfillan' © James Reeves from *Complete Poems for Children* (Faber Finds) is reprinted by permission of the James Reeves Estate. Anthology available at www.faber.co.uk/faberfinds. 'I Luv Me Mudder' by Benjamin Zephaniah (copyright © Benjamin Zephaniah) is reproduced by permission of United Agents (www.unitedagents.co.uk) on behalf of Benjamin Zephaniah.

The publisher and Rosalind Bliss wish to thank the Cowan family for posing for the illustration featured under 'Piano' by D. H. Lawrence.

Where poets are no longer living, their dates are given.

Introduction

The word 'mother' evokes so many feelings – it is one of the most powerful words in the English language. More often than not, mothers mean safety, love, generosity, wisdom, humour and rules that are occasionally honoured in the breach. Mothers, singly and globally, are a deeply emotional subject.

I was once at a wedding where, in the middle of the service, the vicar likened God to a mother hen. That made the congregation sit up, and the image has stayed with me ever since. I am convinced that the mothering instinct – the wish to look after, to protect, to nurture – means that to be a mother you don't have to be a woman or even have children. I can spot a mother a mile off – a doer of good deeds, a spiritual or practical kisser-better, a kindly finger-wagger, a baker of enough cakes to feed all the armies of the world (while wishing there weren't *any* armies so that everyone could eternally be on hand for Sunday lunch).

My own mother, to whom this publication is dedicated, used to say that children bring their parents up, not the other way round. She was a wonderful woman. I spend half my life repeating her sayings to my own children ('worse things happen at sea', 'it will all look better in the morning'). And thus an unbroken chain of wisdom, the wisdom of mothers, ensures that there is always just enough sanity and compassion around to stop the world falling apart.

Jenny Swann

Going out with Mum

'Still got the umbrella dad gave me last Christmas.
Just fetch my gloves dear, no, the leather ones,
The ones I went to Baker Street to collect
And the man said "All change" and wouldn't let me stop
To think if I had everything.
Look in the other drawer. Have you seen my purse, John?
I know I had it. I'd just paid the milkman
And the phone rang. Look in the bathroom then.
Keys, money, letters. Have you got handkerchiefs?
Don't sniff, Bridget, blow. I must make sure
I've got the address right. D'you think you'd better take macs?
Just put the bread knife away dear, you never know
Who may get in and if they see one handy
It might – no, leave the kitchen window
There's the cat.'

We round the corner as the bus pulls off
From the bus stop. 'Now if you'd been ready
We might have caught that. It would have made all the difference.
There might not be another one for hours.'

We almost believe it's true it was our fault:
Mum's too good at being efficient for it to be hers.

Jenny Joseph

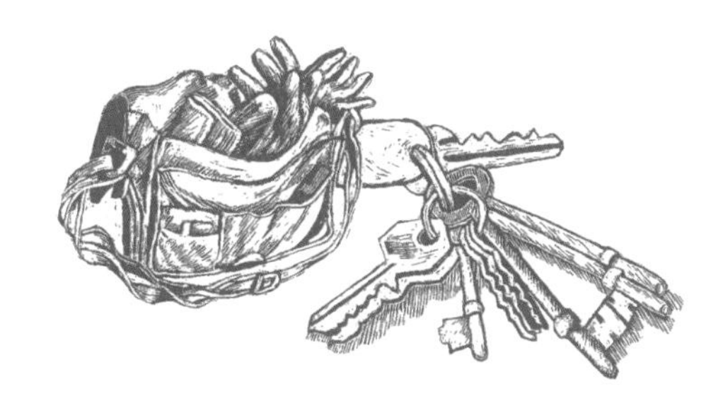

The Habit of Light

In the early evening she liked to switch on the lamps
in corners, on low tables, to show off her brass,
her polished furniture, her silver and glass.
At dawn she'd draw all the curtains back for a glimpse
of the cloud-lit sea. Her oak floors flickered
in an opulence of beeswax and light.
In the kitchen, saucepans danced their lids, the kettle purred
on the Aga, supper on its breath and the buttery melt
of a pie, and beyond the swimming glass of old windows,
in the deep perspective of the garden, a blackbird singing,
she'd come through the bean rows in tottering shoes,
her pinny full of strawberries, a lettuce, bringing
the palest potatoes in a colander, her red hair bright
with her habit of colour, her habit of light.

Gillian Clarke

I Luv Me Mudder

I luv me mudder an me mudder luvs me
    We cum so far from over de sea,
We heard dat de streets were paved wid gold
    Sometimes it's hot, sometimes it's cold,
I luv me mudder an me mudder luvs me
    We try fe live in harmony
Yu might know her as Valerie
    But to me she's just my mummy.

She shouts at me daddy so loud sometime
    She's always been a friend of mine
She's always doing de best she can
    She works so hard down ina Englan,
She's always singin sum kinda song
    She has big muscles an she very, very strong,
She likes pussycats an she luvs cashew nuts
    An she don't bother wid no if an buts.

I luv me mudder an me mudder luvs me
    We come so far from over de sea,
We heard dat de streets were paved wid gold
    Sometimes it's hot, sometimes it's cold,
I luv her and whatever we do
    Dis is a luv I know is true,
My people, I'm talking to yu
    Me an my mudder we luv yu too.

Benjamin Zephaniah

Mrs Gilfillan

When Mrs Gilfillan
  Is troubled with troubles,
She flies to the kitchen
  And sits blowing bubbles.
When Mrs Gilfillan
  Is worried by money,
When her feet are like lead
  And her head's feeling funny,
When there's too much to do
  And the chimney is smoking,
And everything's awkward
  And wrong and provoking,
When the washing won't dry
  For the rain's never ending,
When the cupboards need cleaning
  And stockings want mending,
When the neighbours complain
  Of the noise of the cat,
And she ought to be looking
  For this and for that,
And never a line comes
  From her married daughter –

Then off to the kitchen
  With soap and warm water
Goes Mrs Gilfillan
  And all her troubles;
And she puffs them away
  In a great cloud of bubbles.
In joyful abandon
  She puffs them and blows them,
And all round about her
  In rapture she throws them;
When round, clear and shiny
  They hang in the air,
Away like a shadow
  Goes worry and care.

James Reeves (1909 - 1978)

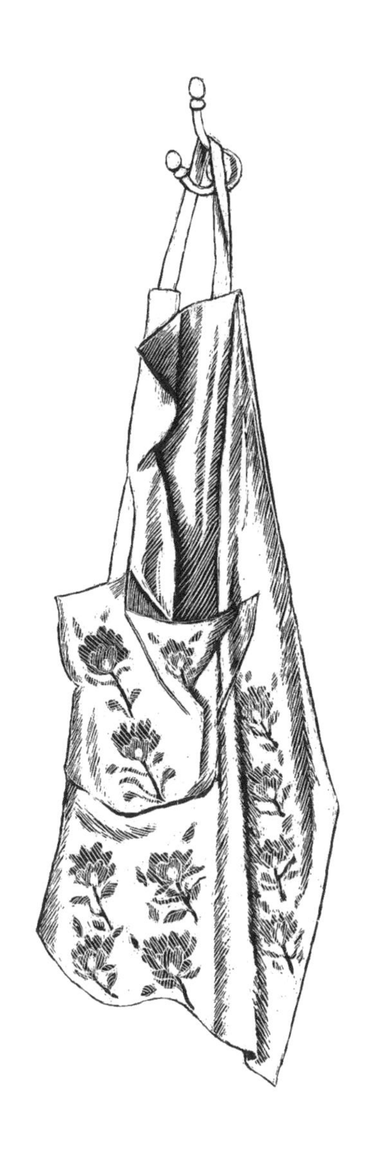

I try my absolute best

I give my kids pure apple juice
(no sugar less acid than orange)
buy my baby soya milk formula
now she's off the breast
(non dairy, no cholesterol, good
for their little hearts – apparently
their arteries can harden before five
even). Water from the purifier.
Perrier if I'm feeling flush
(they can always pretend it's lemonade).
Carob-coated date bars. Cherry or banana.
And there's a shop down the street
that is selling organic vegetables
(no sprays, no chemicals).
Only to find the bloody English apples
are being sprayed with Alar and are
carcinogenic; the soya beans are cooked
in aluminium pots which gives off deposits
in the brain; the cartridge in the purifier
collects things (like knickers if they're not changed).
Perrier's got Benzene in it which gives rats
cancer. Though I personally don't know any rat
that drinks Perrier, do you? And them
so-called Health Food Bars contain more sugar
than the average Mars Bar. What's the use
in calling anything organic when
the bloody soil's chock-a-block with lead?

I try my absolute best,
drink decaff coffee to pipe me down
instead of hype me up only to find
out from my eldest daughter
that what they put the beans through
is worse for you than an ordinary Nescafé.

I'm back on Valium.
My kids are stuffing Monster Munch
and Mars Bars down them.
My youngest son even ate a hamburger yesterday.
It's driving me crazy.
I says it's your pocket money,
Do what you want with it.

Jackie Kay

Human Affection

Mother, I love you so.
Said the child, I love you more than I know.
She laid her head on her mother's arm,
And the love between them kept them warm.

Stevie Smith (1902 - 1971)

To My Mother

Today's your natal day,
Sweet flowers I bring;
Mother, accept, I pray,
My offering.

And may you happy live,
And long us bless;
Receiving as you give
Great happiness.

Christina Rossetti (1830 - 1894)

This was Christina Rossetti's first recorded poem, written when she was eleven years old and given to her mother on 27th April 1842 along with a posy. Her mother noted that "These verses are truly and literally by my little daughter, who scrupulously rejected all assistance in her rhyming efforts, under the impression that in that case they would not really be her own".

Piano

Softly, in the dusk, a woman is singing to me;
Taking me back down the vista of years, till I see
A child sitting under the piano, in the boom of the tingling strings
And pressing the small, poised feet of a mother who smiles as she sings.

In spite of myself, the insidious mastery of song
Betrays me back, till the heart of me weeps to belong
To the old Sunday evenings at home, with winter outside
And hymns in the cosy parlour, the tinkling piano our guide.

So now it is vain for the singer to burst into clamour
With the great black piano appassionato. The glamour
Of childish days is upon me, my manhood is cast
Down in the flood of remembrance, I weep like a child for the past.

D. H. Lawrence (1885 - 1930)

The Chiffonier

You're glad I like the chiffonier. But I
feel suddenly uneasy, scenting why
you're pleased I like this pretty thing you've bought,
the twin of one that stood beside your cot
when you were small; you've marked it down for me;
it's not too heavy to be sent by sea
when the time comes, and it's got space inside
to pack some other things you've set aside,
things that are small enough to go by water
twelve thousand miles to me, your English daughter.
I know your habits – writing all our names
in books and on the backs of picture-frames,
allotting antique glass and porcelain dishes
to granddaughters according to their wishes,
promising me the tinted photograph
of my great-grandmother. We used to laugh,
seeing how each occasional acquisition
was less for you than for later disposition:
'You know how Marilyn likes blue and white
china? I've seen some plates, I thought I might
indulge in.' Bless you, Mother! But we're not
quite so inclined to laugh now that you've got
something that's new to you but not a part
of your estate: that weakness in your heart.
It makes my distance from you, when I go
back home next week, suddenly swell and grow
from thirty hours' flying to a vast
galactic space between present and past.
How many more times can I hope to come
to Wellington and find you still at home?

We've talked about it, as one has to, trying
to see the lighter aspects of your dying:
'You've got another twenty years or more'
I said, 'but when you think you're at death's door
just let me know. I'll come and hang about
for however long it takes to see you out.'
'I don't think it'll be like that' you said:
'I'll pop off suddenly one night in bed.'
How secretive! How satisfying! You'll
sneak off, a kid running away from school –
well, that at least's the only way I find
I can bring myself to see it in my mind.
But now I see you in your Indian skirt
and casual cornflower-blue linen shirt
in the garden, under your feijoa tree,
looking about as old or young as me.
Dear little Mother! Naturally I'm glad
you found a piece of furniture that had
happy associations with your youth;
and yes, I do admire it – that's the truth:
its polished wood and touch of Art Nouveau
appeal to me. But surely you must know
I value this or any other treasure
of yours chiefly because it gives you pleasure.
I have to write this now, while you're still here:
I want my mother, not her chiffonier.

Fleur Adcock

Mirror

In my mother's house
is the friendly mirror,
the only glass in which I look
and think I see myself,
think, yes, that's what
I think I'm like,
that's who I am. The only
glass in which I look and smile.

Just as this baby smiles
at the baby who always
smiles at her, the one in
her mother's arms, the mother
who looks like me, who
smiles at herself in her
mother's mirror, the friendly
mirror in her mother's house.

But if I move to one side
we vanish, the woman I thought
was me, the baby making friends
with herself, we move to one side
and the mirror holds no future, no past,
in its liquid frame, only the corner
of an open window, a bee visiting
the ready flowers of summer.

Maura Dooley